BASIC / NOT BORING
SCIENCE SKILLS

SCIENCE INVESTIGATIONS

Grades 6–8⁺

Inventive Exercises to Sharpen
Skills and Raise Achievement

Series Concept & Development
by Imogene Forte & Marjorie Frank
Exercises by Marjorie Frank

Incentive Publications, Inc.
Nashville, Tennessee

About the cover:
Bound resist, or tie dye, is the most ancient known method
of fabric surface design. The brilliance of the basic tie dye
design on this cover reflects the possibilities that emerge
from the mastery of basic skills.

Illustrated by Kathleen Bullock
Cover art by Mary Patricia Deprez, dba Tye Dye Mary®
Cover design by Marta Drayton, Joe Shibley, and W. Paul Nance
Edited by Charlotte Bosarge

ISBN 0-86530-585-4

PRINTED IN THE UNITED STATES OF AMERICA
www.incentivepublications.com

TABLE OF CONTENTS

PHYSICAL SCIENCE INVESTIGATIONS

CELEBRATE BASIC SCIENCE INVESTIGATIONS SKILLS

Basic does not mean boring! There certainly is nothing dull about . . .
  . . . untangling secrets of hairballs, quicksand, quarks, and spiders.
  . . . spying on strange behaviors of plants and animals.
  . . . lurking beneath the ocean surface with weird creatures.
  . . . figuring out what causes some weird body episodes like hiccupping and snoring.
  . . . finding missing identities for gems and minerals.
  . . . probing the mysteries of the surfs and tides.
  . . . exploring black holes and chasing spectacular storms.
  . . . stalking roller coasters, chemicals, snorkelers, and rock bands.

The idea of celebrating the basics is just what it sounds like—enjoying and getting good at knowing how to search for fascinating information in the world of science. Each page invites learners to try a high-interest, appealing exercise that will send them tracking down information and explanations for some event or process in the natural world. This is not just another ordinary fill-in-the-blanks way to learn. These investigations are fun and surprising. Students will do the useful work of deepening science knowledge while they "play detective" to answer some compelling questions.

The pages in this book can be used in many ways:
  • to increase science learning and independent research for one student
  • to expand the whole group's skills at locating and processing science information
  • as the basis for a lesson or unit within the classroom
  • by students working on their own or working under the direction of a parent or teacher

Each page may be used to introduce a new area to explore. Beyond the nineteen investigations, you will find an appendix of resources helpful to the student and teacher—including a glossary of terms used in the book and a ready-to-use test for assessing the material discovered in the investigations.

The pages are written with the assumption that an adult will be available to assist the student with his or her learning. These are not science experiments, such as would be done in a lab. These are research activities. Therefore, it is essential that students have access to science resources, textbooks, encyclopedias, library books, and Internet reference sources.

As your students take on the challenges of these adventures with science facts, concepts, and processes, they will grow. As you watch them check off the science skills they have sharpened, you can celebrate with them!

The Skills Test (pages 56–59)
  Use the skills test as a pretest and/or a post-test. This will help you check the students' mastery of basic skills and understandings gained during the investigations. It can also prepare them for success on tests of standards, instructional goals, or other individual achievement.

SKILLS CHECKLIST FOR SCIENCE INVESTIGATIONS

✔	SKILL	PAGE(S)
	Research to find answers to questions and solutions to problems	10–50
	Show understanding of the system of classification of life	14, 15
	Identify some features of plants and plant behavior	16, 17
	Identify some features of animals and animal behavior	18, 19
	Identify the functions of human body parts	20, 21
	Explain some human body processes	22, 23
	Identify treatments for some body disorders and diseases	24, 25
	Show understanding of some of Earth's internal processes	26, 27
	Show understanding of some of the processes that change Earth's surface	28, 29
	Use physical characteristics to identify some common minerals	30, 31
	Show understanding of the ocean processes related to waves, currents, and tides	32, 33
	Identify different kinds of storms and other weather patterns	34, 35
	Identify some features of space	36, 37
	Recognize features of the different planets	38, 39
	Identify common chemical compounds and their formulas	40, 41
	Show understanding of concepts of force, motion, energy, and matter	42, 43, 44, 45
	Show understanding of how sound is produced and how it travels	46, 47
	Identify common elements and their symbols	48–50
	Show understanding of the Periodic Table	48–50

SCIENCE INVESTIGATIONS

Skills Exercises

Investigation # 1: Unraveling
TRICKY SCIENCE MYSTERIES

It will take sharp detecting to solve these science mysteries—solve them with the help of the Internet. Find the solution to each mystery. Then write the address of the website that helped you with the answer. (Use your favorite search engine to find websites, or use some of the sites listed on page 13.)

1. Do spiders have good eyesight?

Answer _____

_____

Web Address _____

2. Why is the sky blue?

Answer _____

_____

_____

_____

Web Address _____

3. What comet is currently visible from some spot on earth?

Answer _____

_____

Web Address _____

4. How can you tell an acid from a base?

Answer _____

_____

_____

Web Address _____

5. What good is a vacuole?

Answer _____

_____

Web Address _____

6. What does an epidemiologist study?

Answer _____

_____

Web Address _____

7. Can you get pfiesteria from eating shellfish?

Answer _____

Web Address _____

Use with pages 11, 12, and 13.

Name _____

8. **Why do cats cough up hairballs?**

Answer _____

_____

Web Address _____

13. **Could California fall into the Pacific Ocean during a bad earthquake?**

Answer _____

Web Address _____

9. **Of what material are fingernails made?**

Answer _____

Web Address _____

14. **Who are the llama's closest relatives?**

Answer _____

_____

Web Address _____

10. **How old are the oldest coral reefs?**

Answer _____

_____

Web Address _____

15. **Why don't satellites fall from the sky?**

Answer _____

_____

_____

Web Address _____

11. **What should you do if you get caught in quicksand?**

Answer _____

_____

_____

Web Address _____

12. **How many times does a heart beat in an average lifetime?**

Answer _____

Web Address _____

16. **Where would you find a quark?**

Answer _____

_____

Web Address _____

Use with pages 10, 12, and 13.

Name

17. **Why is it easier to float in salt water than in fresh water?**

Answer _____

_____

_____

_____

Web Address _____

18. **What is the Coriolis effect?**

Answer _____

_____

_____

Web Address _____

19. **How is an aurora borealis different from an aurora australis?**

Answer _____

_____

_____

Web Address _____

20. **Where, in the U.S., could you find a black swallowtail butterfly?**

Answer _____

_____

Web Address _____

21. **What is the difference between fission and fusion?**

Answer _____

_____

_____

_____

Web Address _____

22. **Why do bubbles burst so easily?**

Answer _____

_____

_____

Web Address _____

23. **How much water is on Earth?**

Answer _____

_____

Web Address _____

24. **What is granite good for?**

Answer _____

_____

_____

Web Address _____

Use with pages 10, 11, and 13.

Name

These websites can help you find solutions to the science mysteries on pages 10–12.

Aquatic Network – Aquatic World — www.aquanet.com

Ask an Expert — www.cln.org/int_expert.html

Ask Dr. Universe — www.wsu.edu/DrUniverse

The Aurora Page — www.geo.mtu.edu/weather/aurora

Biology Learning Center – Marine Biology — www.marinebiology.org/science.htm

Butterflies.com — www.butterflies.com

Cool Science for Curious Kids — www.hhmi.org/coolscience

Discovery Channel On-Line — www.discovery.com

Earth Kids – Earth Science for Kids/NASA — kids.earth.nasa.gov

The Exploratorium — www.exploratorium.edu

Fear of Physics — www.fearofphysics.com

The Franklin Institute Science Museum — sln.fi.edu

The Heart Online — www.sln.fi.edu/biosci/biosci.html

National Institute of Environmental Health Services — www.niehs.nih.gov/

National Science Foundation — www.nsf.gov/

Oceanlink — www.oceanlink.island.net

Rader's Chem4Kids — www.chem4kids.com

Rader's Kapili.com — www.kapili.com/topiclist.html

Rader's Geography for Kids — www.geography4kids.com

Reeko's Mad Science Lab — www.spartechsoftware.com/reeko

Science Made Simple — www.sciencemadesimple.com

Sea & Sky — www.seasky.org/

Smithsonian Museums — www.si.edu

Space Kids – Space Science for Kids/NASA — spacekids.hq.nasa.gov

U.S. Geological Survey – California Earthquakes — quake.wr.usgs.gov

U.S. Geological Survey Water Science for Schools — ga.water.usgs.gov/edu

Whale Songs — www.whalesongs.org

Yuckiest Site on the Internet — yucky.kids.discovery.com

NOTE: The Internet changes daily. Websites on this page have been chosen carefully; however, a teacher or parent should review sites before directing students to the site.

Use with pages 10, 11, and 12.

Investigation #2: Getting to Know
WHO'S WHO IN THE KINGDOMS

A one-celled organism appears in your microscope. Could it belong to the plant kingdom? Another organism, with a two-chambered heart, appears in your kitchen. Could it belong to the monerans kingdom? Use your knowledge of life classification and good investigative tools to make some identifications for these:

Organism #1 lives on the land and produces seeds and flowers. Could it be an angiosperm? _____

Name its kingdom. _____

Organism #4 is a bacteria—a one-celled organism with no nucleus. It has a cell wall and a flagellum for movement.

Name its kingdom. _____

Organism #7 has a body divided into two main regions. It has a hard exoskeleton, jointed legs, and two pairs of antennae. Could it be a crustacean? _____

Name its phylum. _____

_____

Name its kingdom. _____

Organism #2 is a horsetail. It makes its own food, and reproduces with spores found in structures that look like pine cones. Is it an algae? _____

Name its kingdom. _____

Organism #5 has a tube-shaped body divided into segments. Its many bristles help its movement. Could it belong to the phylum Annelida? _____

Name its kingdom. _____

Organism #8 also has a segmented body and a hard exoskeleton. But it has three divisions, one pair of antennae, three pairs of jointed legs, and wings. Could it be an insect? _____

Name its phylum. _____

_____

Name its kingdom. _____

Organism #3 has the name haliclona. It has no symmetry and no tissues. Cells form inner and outer layers around a central cavity. Name its phylum. _____

Name its kingdom. _____

Organism #6 All of these organisms except one belong to the same phylum.
jellyfish   anemone
hydra   fluke
                    coral
Name the phylum. _____

Name the kingdom. _____

Use with page 15.

Name _____

Organism #9
is a euglenoid—a one-celled organism that can make its own food. It lives in fresh water and moves with the help of flagella.

Name its kingdom.

_____

Organism #14
is an Adder's-tongue. It is one of a group of many-celled, vascular organisms. It has fronds, which hold the spore cases that help the plant reproduce.

Name its phylum.

_____

Name its kingdom.

_____

Organism #12
All of these organisms except one belong to the same phylum.

sea urchin   sea cucumber
starfish   clam

Name the phylum. _____

Name the kingdom. _____
Which organism does not belong?

_____

Organism #10
is a fuzzy creature with eight legs, a body with two segments, an exoskeleton, and no antennae. It shares a class with mites and ticks.

Name its class. _____

Name its phylum. _____

Name its kingdom.

_____

Organism #15
is called a Death Cap. It cannot make its own food. It reproduces by forming spores in a club-shaped sac. While some organisms in this group are helpful or edible, this organism is deadly.

Name its kingdom.

_____

Organism #13
has the scientific name _Vulpez zerda_. (This names its genus and species.) Dogs and wolves belong to the same family, Canidae.

Name its order. _____

Name its class. _____

Name its phylum. _____

Name its kingdom.

_____

Organism #11
is a hookworm, a parasite that infects humans by living in the intestine.

Name its phylum.

_____

Name its kingdom.

_____

Organism #16
is an octopus, the most intelligent member of its phylum. Which other organisms belong to the same phylum? _(Circle them.)_
snail   slug   jellyfish
squid   oyster   clam

Name its phylum. _____

Name its kingdom.

_____

Use with page 14.

Name _____

Investigation #3: Tracking Down
WILD & WACKY PLANTS

Find out about the weird behaviors and odd characteristics of some of
the strangest plants on the earth! Read about each plant. Then track
down the missing information.

1. The largest known flower in the world has an odd name. It is called
   the **corpse flower**. Maybe this name comes from its terrible smell
   of rotten fish. Another strange thing about this flower is the
   blooming schedule. Find out how often it blooms.

   _____

2. The **horsetail** has been around since the time of dinosaurs. It is a
   strange-looking plant because it has no branches, leaves, or flowers.
   It is just a tall stalk with a cone-shaped structure on top. Early
   Americans used horsetails to scour their pots and pans or to polish
   wood. Find out what the horsetail contains that makes the plant a
   good, scratchy (abrasive) tool.

   _____

3. The **Venus Fly Trap** is the most famous of the weird plants.
   It is known for its carnivorous behavior. Find out how the plant
   traps flies.

   _____

4. The **Tropical Pitcher Plant** has a shape like a pitcher. This helps
   the plant gobble up bugs for dinner. Find out how the bugs are
   lured into the plant.

   _____

5. A tiny, tiny plant called **Wolffia** has the tiniest flower and tiniest
   fruit in the world. The fruit weighs about the same as a grain of salt.
   It takes about 20–30 of the plants to fill a square inch. The plant has
   flat, oval-shaped leaves, and grows without real roots. Find out the
   common name for this plant. Where is it found?

   _____

6. There is something very unusual about the **Coco De Mer**, an
   endangered palm tree. It is not the tree itself that is unusual.
   It is not the flower. It is something about the seed. What can
   you find out about the seed of this plant? (Its botanical name is
   Lodoicea maldivica.)

   _____

Use with page 17.

Name _____

16

7. **Indian Pipes** look like ghosts because they are completely white. These plants have no chlorophyll so they cannot make their own food. Find out how Indian Pipes find food.

   _____

8. The **African Witch Weed** has a big problem. It can live on its own for only about a week. Find out what it does to stay alive.

   _____

9. The **Traveler's Palm** looks like a palm tree, but it is actually a member of the banana family. It is called the Traveler's Palm because it can offer water to quench the thirst of travelers. Find out how this tree holds water.

   _____

10. A **Carrion Flower** has a very strange characteristic. It looks like a balloon before it opens. Then, when it opens, it looks like a starfish. But this is not the strange thing. The most "outstanding" characteristic of the Carrion Flower is its terrible smell of rotting meat. Find out what this horrible smell accomplishes for the flower.

    _____

11. The **Coryanthes orchid** has a very unusual shape. A certain kind of wasp sometimes falls into this strange shape and gets drenched with the liquid it holds. The wet wasp cannot fly out of the plant; to exit, it must crawl through a narrow tunnel. This very odd plant has an "arm" that holds the wasp while it deposits pollen on the creature. Then the wasp is allowed to crawl out and fly away, loaded with pollen! Describe the flower's unusual shape.

    _____

12. **Strangler Figs** are plants with a nasty habit. Find out why these are called "stranglers."

    _____

13. The **Compass plant** has an unusual talent. What is this talent?

    _____

14. The **Rose of Jericho** practices an odd behavior. It dries up, curling its stems into a tight ball. Then it rolls around in the wind, dropping its seeds across the land. The Rose of Jericho is also known as a resurrection plant. Explain what this means.

    _____

Use with page 16.

Name

17

Investigation #4: Stalking
MONSTERS OF THE DEEP

Search out information to learn about these scary-looking deep sea creatures. Find out which creatures match the descriptions below. Write one or more letters for each answer.

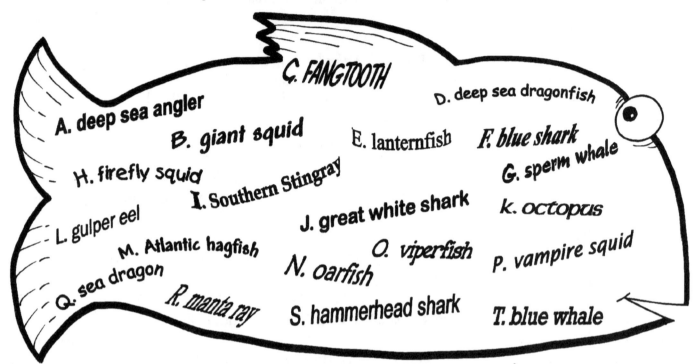

C. FANGTOOTH

D. deep sea dragonfish

A. deep sea angler

B. giant squid

E. lanternfish

F. blue shark

H. firefly squid

G. sperm whale

I. Southern Stingray

L. gulper eel

J. great white shark

k. octopus

M. Atlantic hagfish

O. viperfish

P. vampire squid

Q. sea dragon

N. oarfish

R. manta ray

S. hammerhead shark

T. blue whale

_____ 1. 4 or more creatures that spend time 1000 feet or deeper beneath the surface

_____ 2. a creature that produces huge amounts of slime to protect itself

_____ 3. creatures that use light-producing features to lure prey

_____ 4. a powerful, sharp-beaked, tentacled creature not generally found alive in the wild

_____ 5. the largest animal on earth

_____ 6. the longest bony fish in the ocean, also known as a ribbonfish

_____ 7. a graceful animal with a 15–20 ft. wingspan; scary, but harmless to people

_____ 8. a creature with an enormous mouth and long sharp teeth, who lives at 16,000-foot depths

_____ 9. a creature with a bizarre, pelican-like mouth and a tail like a whip

_____ 10. a creature that holds its breath to dive to depths of up to 10,000 feet for food

_____ 11. the fastest shark in the ocean

_____ 12. a creature that looks like seaweed and has a scary name, but is not fierce

Use with page 19.

Name

Which statements about "monsters of the deep" are **true**? Circle their numbers.
Then, investigate and answer questions A and B.

1. Sharks are mammals.

2. Sharks have no bones.

3. All sharks are predators.

4. Sharkskin is soft and smooth.

5. Only some sharks are carnivores.

6. All sharks are dangerous to humans.

7. Sharks have a keen sense of smell.

8. Sharks are closely related to rays.

9. A ray is actually a flattened shark.

10. Octopuses and squids have red blood.

11. A Southern Stingray is harmless to humans.

12. The Great White Shark can be as long as 25 feet.

13. Sharks are constantly losing and renewing teeth.

14. Squids live in dens near the floor of the ocean.

15. Rays and sharks both belong to the bony fish class.

16. Most adult octopuses and squids die after reproducing.

17. Octopuses and squids move by a system of jet propulsion.

18. Sharks are found only in the Atlantic and Pacific Oceans.

19. A shark gets some of its buoyancy from a large, oily liver.

20. The most important sense a shark uses to detect its prey is sight.

21. All sharks spend most of their time very deep in the ocean
    (below 1500 feet).

22. A hammerhead shark is one of the aggressive species known
    to attack humans.

23. A Lesser Electric Ray can deliver a powerful electric shock as high as 30 volts.

24. Octopuses and squids can protect themselves by squirting a stream of dark ink
    at a predator.

A.
What is dangerous about the *lionfish?*

_____

_____

_____

B.
What is dangerous about the
Moray eel?

_____

_____

_____

_____

Use with page 18.

Name _____

Investigation #5: Scrutinizing
WEIRD & WONDERFUL BODY PARTS

Five doctors are taking part in some research. Their names are: Dr. B. J. Renal, Dr. L. Bowe, Dr. S. Turnam, Dr. G. Larynx, and Dr. A. Orta. Each has been asked to scrutinize five different body parts or substances. (These are not necessarily the areas that each doctor would ordinarily study in his or her field.) The pictures are labeled with the doctors' blood types.

Read the clues on the next page. Use them to help discover which doctor is which, and what each is studying. Write their names in the correct places. Also write the names of the body parts or substances being studied by each doctor. (See the five lines in each box.)

1.
a. _____
b. _____
c. _____
d. _____
e. _____

Dr._____ Endocrinologist   blood type O+

2.
a. _____
b. _____
c. _____
d. _____
e. _____

Dr._____ Oncologist   blood type B+

3.
a. _____
b. _____
c. _____
d. _____
e. _____

Dr._____ Hematologist   blood type A

4.
a. _____
b. _____
c. _____
d. _____
e. _____

Dr._____ Podiatrist   blood type B-

5.
a. _____
b. _____
c. _____
d. _____
e. _____

Dr._____ Cytologist   blood type AB+

Use with page 21.

Name

Clues

1. Dr. S. Turnam's parents both have Rh-negative blood.
2. Dr. G. Larynx has a blood type known as the "universal donor."
3. Dr. L. Bowe's lifelong work involves studying cancer.
4. Dr. B. J. Renal can receive blood from any other blood type donor.
5. The doctor who specializes in cell study has been asked to investigate an organ behind the stomach that filters blood and stores extra blood for emergencies. He also is looking at the long branches of nerve cells.
6. The doctor who studies feet is now looking at the eye muscle that regulates pupil size. This doctor also will look at the five long bones in the foot.
7. Dr. Bowe is examining a hard layer of the tooth that protects the tooth's center, and a gland that secretes a substance to regulate glucose.
8. The doctor who can receive only type O blood investigates an organ that stores bile, and a nerve that carries sound signals to the brain.
9. The doctor who is studying the large muscles at the sides and front of the abdomen can donate blood only to persons with type AB or type B blood.
10. Dr. Renal is studying the largest salivary gland.
11. The doctor who can receive blood only from type O or A studies the large veins on either side of the neck that bring carbon dioxide-laden blood from the head to the heart. This doctor also studies the structures in blood that form blood clots.
12. The doctor who studies feet is examining the part of the brain that regulates heartbeat. This doctor also looks at the substance that gives skin its color.
13. The doctor whose field is the study of blood now examines the calf muscle.
14. Dr. Larynx examines an iron-containing red pigment in red blood cells and the large nerves that run down the legs. (These nerves sometimes get pinched when the back is injured.)
15. Dr. Renal studies the lower chambers of the heart, and a substance released by the liver that breaks up fats.
16. Dr. Turnam is studying the shoulder muscle.
17. The doctor who ordinarily studies tumors is now examining the gland in the upper chest which functions to fight infection.
18. The doctor who specializes in hormones is now studying a gland in the neck. This gland regulates the rate at which the body produces energy for food.
19. The hematologist is studying tubes that carry ovum from the ovaries to the uterus. She also investigates the two tubes carrying oxygen from the trachea into the lungs.
20. Dr. Bowe is studying the large, wide, flat bone of the pelvis.

Use with page 20.

Name

Investigation #6: Explaining
STRANGE BODY EPISODES

Strange things are happening around Dr. Wilma Wiggle's body. These are body processes that just happen-sometimes she cannot even control them. Tell what is happening in each "incident."

1. While Wilma Wiggle was sleeping, oil, tears, and sweat were dripping down from tubes in her eyes. This stuff collected near her carnucles. What has happened?

   _____

2. Wilma is giving a speech at an important meeting when a nerve that controls her diaphragm suddenly stimulates it, and her diaphragm contracts without warning. This keeps happening over and over, and she keeps sucking in air quickly, which causes her epiglottis to snap shut suddenly. She cannot stop this from happening. Wilma gets terribly embarrassed about the repeated noises and interruptions in her speech. Finally, she has to leave the meeting. What is happening?

   _____

3. Wilma has been swallowing gases (mostly air). Suddenly, some of the gas escapes quickly from her stomach and travels up through her esophagus and out through her mouth. She is embarrassed by the sound. What is happening?

   _____

4. Something has irritated the lining of Wilma's sinus passages. She tries to ignore it, but her body can't. Without her permission, nerve endings are stimulated and she suddenly expels air quickly from her nose and mouth. A lot of other stuff, like moisture and mucus, is also expelled. So, she's embarrassed again. What's happened?

   _____

5. Thousands of dead skin cells have gotten mixed with the oozing oil from Wilma's hair follicles. These dead skin cells and dirt from the air have combined into a messy gunk. The flakes of this gunk are breaking off and falling onto her shoulders. What is happening?

   _____

6. It has been a long meeting, and the air is stuffy. Dr. Wiggle has fallen asleep. Somehow the flow of air through the passages at the back of her mouth and nose got obstructed. Structures in the back of her throat strike each other and vibrate when she breathes. This makes another embarrassing sound. But, since she is asleep, she doesn't hear it! What is happening?

   _____

Use with page 23.

Name

Conduct more investigations to see if you can explain other strange body happenings. For each of these "episodes" describe what the body is actually doing.

A. skin wrinkling in the bathtub

B. a funny "funny bone" feeling

C. a yawn

D. bad breath

E. ears popping on an airplane

F. a shiver

G. earwax

Use with page 22.

Name

Investigation #7: Delving Into
DISTURBING DISORDERS

Dr. Cam B. Kurred sees a seemingly endless line of patients with disturbing disorders and diseases. He has to make judgments every day about treatments for the patients.

Survey the list of diseases and disorders on this page and the next page. Do some investigating to learn about treatments for these ailments. Choose and circle or underline 15 ailments. For each one, suggest one or two possible options for treatment. If you suggest medicines or drugs, try to describe specific kinds of drugs that could be used.

AILMENTS

acne	asthma		fainting	
AIDS	athlete's foot	chicken pox	fever	hepatitis
allergies	botulism	dehydration	fracture	hypothermia
anthrax	broken bones	depression	fungus	impetigo
anxiety	bronchitis	diabetes	gastroenteritis	influenza
appendicitis	cancer	earache	heart disease	insect stings
arthritis	cavity	exhaustion	heat stroke	

1. Disease/disorder _____

   Treatment(s) _____

   _____

2. Disease/disorder _____

   Treatment(s) _____

   _____

3. Disease/disorder _____

   Treatment(s) _____

   _____

4. Disease/disorder _____

   Treatment(s) _____

   _____

5. Disease/disorder _____

   Treatment(s) _____

   _____

Some Treatment Ideas
decongestants
liquids
vaccine
radiation
surgery
casting
antibiotics
immobilization
aspirin
antiseptics
rest
antihistamines
a cool bath
transplant
inhaler

Use with page 25.

Name _____

AILMENTS

kidney disease
laryngitis
lead poisoning
malaria
measles
meningitis
mumps
pneumonia
poison ivy
pyorrhea
rabies
roseola
scarlet fever
schizophrenia
shock
smallpox
snake bite
sprain
strep throat
stroke
tetanus
torn ligaments
tuberculosis
typhoid

6. Disease/disorder _____
   Treatment(s) _____
   _____
7. Disease/disorder _____
   Treatment(s) _____
   _____
8. Disease/disorder _____
   Treatment(s) _____
   _____
9. Disease/disorder _____
   Treatment(s) _____
   _____
10. Disease/disorder _____
    Treatment(s) _____
    _____
11. Disease/disorder_____
    Treatment(s) _____
    _____
12. Disease/disorder _____
    Treatment(s) _____
    _____
13. Disease/disorder _____
    Treatment(s) _____
    _____
14. Disease/disorder _____
    Treatment(s) _____
    _____
15. Disease/disorder _____
    Treatment(s) _____
    _____

More Treatment Ideas to Use for Both Pages
chemotherapy
blood thinning drugs
dialysis
physical therapy
medicine
cleaning wounds
exercise
change in diet
physical therapy
change of residence
removal of irritant
steroids
desensitization
quarantine

Use with page 24.

Name

Investigation #8: Exploring
EARTH'S RUMBLES, RATTLES, & ROLLS

Follow that scientist! Geologist Sylvester S. Izmic spends his life figuring out the bubblings and groanings, eruptions, quivers, and quakes of the earth. Look at his list of earth "antics" to investigate. Keep your own log book, with a brief explanation for each Earth event or feature. **_What makes it happen?_**

1. seismic waves

2. a strato-volcano

3. a caldera

4. a fault

5. a dome volcano

6. hot springs

7. folding in rocks

8. a shield volcano

Is the ground moving?

9. a geyser

Use with page 27.

Name

Use your good investigative skills to learn about some of history's major earthquakes. Then finish the log that Dr. Izmic began.

Some Deadly Earthquakes of the Twentieth Century

"Oops!"

	Date	Location	Estimate of Deaths	Magnitude of Quake
1	Apr 18–19, 1906	San Francisco, CA, USA		
2	Dec 28, 1908	Messina, Italy		
3	Dec 16, 1920			
4	Sept 1, 1923	Yokohama, Japan		
5	May 22, 1927	Nan-Shan, China		
6	Dec 25, 1932			
7	May 30, 1935			
8	Oct 5, 1948	Turkmenistan, USSR		
9	Mar 27, 1964	Alaska, USA		
10	May 31, 1970	Yungay, Peru		
11	Feb 4, 1976	Guatemala		
12	Jul 28, 1976			
13	Dec 7, 1988	Armenia		
14	Oct 17, 1989			
15	Jun 21, 1990	Iran		
16	Jan 17, 1994	Northridge, CA, USA		
17	Jan 16, 1995			
18	May 30, 1998	Northeast Afghanistan		
19	Aug 17, 1999	Turkey		
20	Jan 26, 2001	Gujarat, India		

21. What, exactly, is an earthquake?

_____

_____

_____

_____

_____.

Use with page 26.

Name

Investigation #9: Looking For
CHANGES—SWIFT & SLOW

Earth is always changing. If you blink your eyes, you might miss a quick change. If you stare all day, some changes might be happening right before your eyes—too slow for you to see.

Four things change Earth's surface: the wind, moving water, gravity, and ice. They are each very powerful. Do you know what they can do to the Earth?

What can wind do?

1. Wind can pick up loose material from the ground surface and move it. This process is called _____ .

2. Wind can carry particles along and "sandblast" rock surfaces, polishing or pitting them. This process is called

   _____ .

3. Wind can pick up material from one spot and deposit it somewhere else. The deposited material is called _____ .

4. _____ , the most common wind deposits, are formed when wind full of blowing sand drops the sand as it blows across an obstacle.

What can gravity do?

5. Gravity pulls loose material down slopes. Material that collects at the foot of a steep slope or cliff is called

   _____ .

6. In a _____ , large amounts of rock loosen and fall.

7. _____ are caused when large amounts of material slide quickly down slopes.

8. Soil and other material from weathering mixed with rain can move rapidly down a slope, causing a

   _____ .

9. Sometimes materials move so slowly that the movement cannot be seen. This is called _____ .

Use with page 29.

Name _____

What can moving water do?

10. Moving water running off soil and slopes, carries dirt and debris, and leaves it in apron-shaped deposits called _____ .

11. Moving water in a river or stream can pick up sediment and carry it along in a _____ load, or drag heavy material along, scraping the river bottom. This load is a _____ load.

12. During a flood, a river carries large amounts of sediment. When it spills over its banks, the river drops the heaviest sediment along the edge, forming a ridge called a _____ . Fine sediment is carried farther from the river channel and dropped to form a _____ .

13. A river usually deposits sediment at its mouth in the shape of a fan. This deposit is called a _____ .

14. Groundwater seeping into limestone regions can dissolve the stone. This can create openings in the bedrock, called _____ . If a "roof" is left when an area is dissolved, a _____ bridge might remain. Funnel-shaped depressions beneath the surface, left when the rock dissolves, become dangerous _____ .

What can ice do?

15. In a process called _____ , a glacier (moving ice) scours the bedrock as it moves. It leaves long scratches, or _____ , on the rock.

16. In another process, called _____ , the moving glacier picks up debris and moves it along to other places.

17. When the glacier melts or recedes, it drops this debris (called _____) into piles around the edges. These piles are _____ .

Use with page 28.

Name _____

Investigation #10: Confirming
MISSING IDENTITIES

This adventuresome scientist has located several interesting mineral specimens. She knows all about the characteristics of the minerals, because she has been examining them closely. Now she needs to know their names. Find the missing identities. Write the name of each mineral on its label. (See list of minerals on the next page.)

Rocks are so exciting!

Specimen #1

_____

color: white
crystals: cubic
luster: nonmetallic
hardness: fingernail can scratch it; it cannot scratch a penny
streak: colorless
other: salty

Specimen #2

_____

color: red
crystals: dodecahedron
luster: nonmetallic
hardness: can scratch glass but not topaz
streak: colorless

Specimen #3

_____

color: brassy yellow
crystals: cubic
luster: metallic
hardness: 6.5
streak: greenish-black

Specimen #4

_____

color: colorless or white
crystals: hexagonal
luster: nonmetallic
hardness: can be scratched by a fingernail
streak: colorless or white

Specimen #5

_____

color: white
crystals: monoclinic
luster: nonmetallic
hardness: 2
streak: white

Specimen #6

_____

color: colorless
crystals: hexagonal
luster: nonmetallic
hardness: can scratch feldspar; can be scratched by garnet
streak: colorless

Specimen #7

_____

color: silver grey
crystals: cubic
luster: metallic
hardness: can be scratched by a penny, but not by a fingernail
streak: grey

Specimen #8

_____

color: yellow
crystals: prismatic
luster: nonmetallic
hardness: scratches garnet
streak: colorless
other: very dense

Use with page 31.

Name

silver   garnet
gold   graphite   galea
sulfur   copper
corundum
topaz   quartz   magnetite   calcite
diamond   halite   pyrite
talc   bauxite
gypsum

ROCK HOUND

Specimen #11

color: copper red
crystals: cubic
luster: metallic
hardness: 3
streak: copper red

Specimen #14

color: greenish-white
crystals: monoclinic
luster: nonmetallic
hardness: 1
streak: white
other: soapy feel

Specimen #9

color: blue
crystals: hexagonal
luster: nonmetallic
hardness: scratches topaz
streak: white

Specimen #12

color: yellow
crystals: orthorhombic
luster: nonmetallic
hardness: can scratch glass
             but not topaz
streak: colorless
other: strong odor when
         wet

Specimen #15

color: colorless
crystals: isometric
luster: nonmetallic
hardness: can scratch all
             other minerals
streak: white
other: brilliant luster

Specimen #10

color: black
crystals: hexagonal
luster: metallic
hardness: can be scratched
             by a fingernail
streak: black
other: flaky, leaves fingers
         black

Specimen #13

color: black
crystals: cubic
luster: metallic
hardness: 6
streak: black

Specimen #16

color: silver
crystals: cubic
luster: metallic
hardness: cannot scratch
             a penny
streak: silvery grey

Use with page 30.

Name

Investigation #11: Untangling
SECRETS OF MOVING WATERS

What secrets lie tossed about in the waves or rising and falling with the tides? Do you know them?

The water of the ocean is constantly in motion. What makes it move? Search for the information that will untangle the mysteries of moving waters. When you find it, write the answers that tell the secrets.

1. **The secret of surface currents:** *What causes them?*

2. **The secret of density currents:** *What causes them?*

3. **The secret of waves:** *What causes them?*

4. **The circle secret:** *How do water particles move in a wave?*

5. **The secret of waves:** *How is a deep-water wave different from a shallow-water wave?*

6. **The secret of breaking waves:** *What causes a wave to break?*

7. **The secret of surf:** *What causes it?*

8. **The secret of surfing:** *How can a surfer ride a wave?*

Use with page 33.

Name

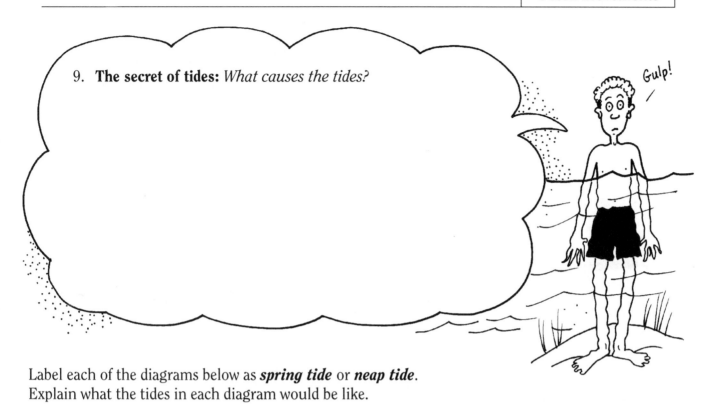

9. **The secret of tides:** *What causes the tides?*

Label each of the diagrams below as ***spring tide*** or ***neap tide***.
Explain what the tides in each diagram would be like.

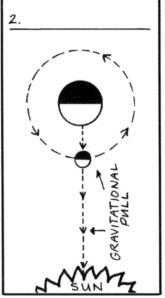
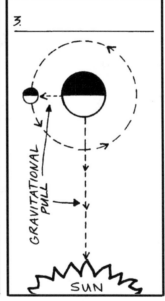
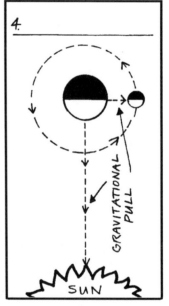

_____

_____

_____

_____

Use with page 32.

Name

Investigation #12: Chasing Down
WILD WEATHER & SPECTACULAR STORMS

Meteorologist Dr. Gail Storm is always caught up in some wild weather. She just can't keep away from any storm or other form of inclement weather!

Here are some of her diary entries from the past few months. For each weather predicament she names, write the details to show that you, too, are savvy about storms and wild weather. (Briefly describe what conditions would be present in that weather situation.)

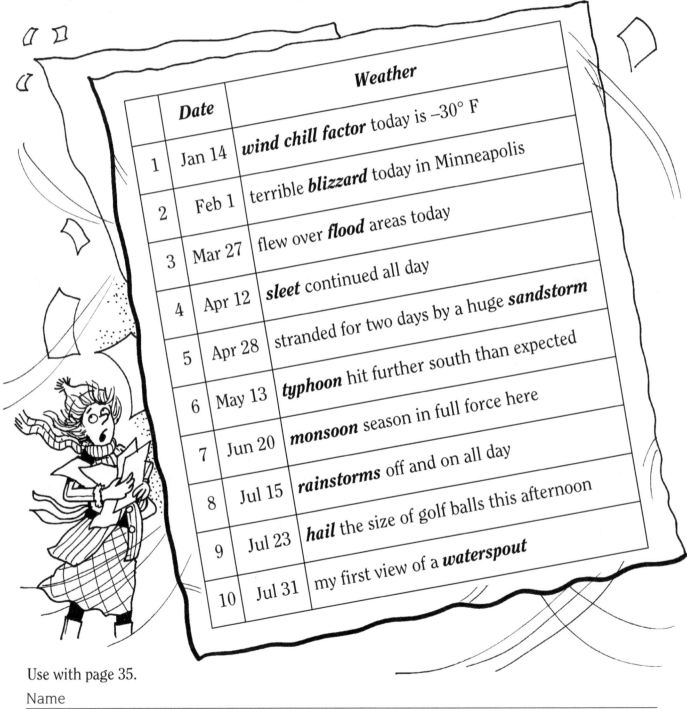

	Date	Weather
1	Jan 14	**wind chill factor** today is –30° F
2	Feb 1	terrible **blizzard** today in Minneapolis
3	Mar 27	flew over **flood** areas today
4	Apr 12	**sleet** continued all day
5	Apr 28	stranded for two days by a huge **sandstorm**
6	May 13	**typhoon** hit further south than expected
7	Jun 20	**monsoon** season in full force here
8	Jul 15	**rainstorms** off and on all day
9	Jul 23	**hail** the size of golf balls this afternoon
10	Jul 31	my first view of a **waterspout**

Use with page 35.

Name

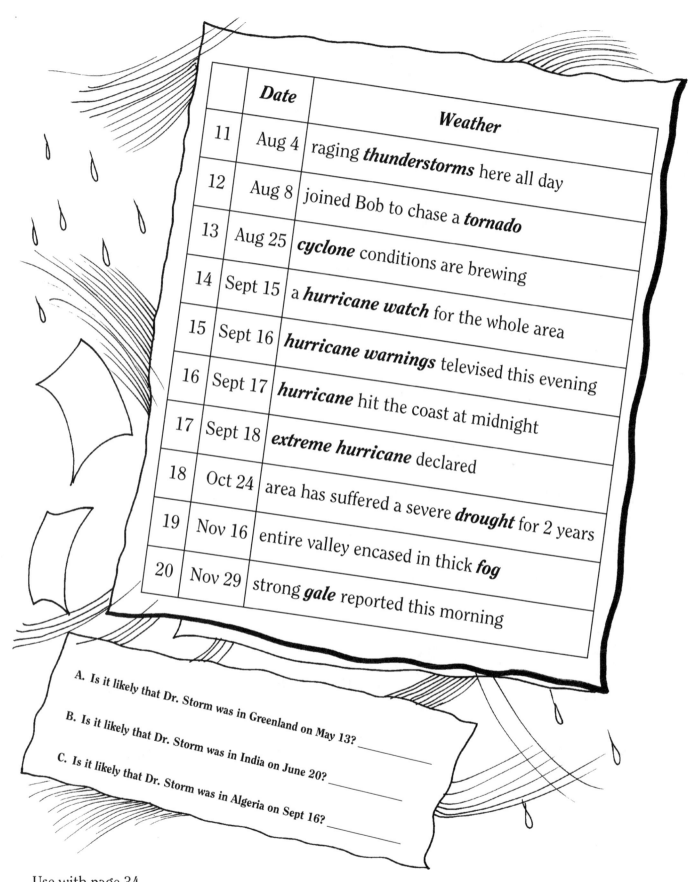

	Date	Weather
11	Aug 4	raging **thunderstorms** here all day
12	Aug 8	joined Bob to chase a **tornado**
13	Aug 25	**cyclone** conditions are brewing
14	Sept 15	a **hurricane watch** for the whole area
15	Sept 16	**hurricane warnings** televised this evening
16	Sept 17	**hurricane** hit the coast at midnight
17	Sept 18	**extreme hurricane** declared
18	Oct 24	area has suffered a severe **drought** for 2 years
19	Nov 16	entire valley encased in thick **fog**
20	Nov 29	strong **gale** reported this morning

A. Is it likely that Dr. Storm was in Greenland on May 13? _____

B. Is it likely that Dr. Storm was in India on June 20? _____

C. Is it likely that Dr. Storm was in Algeria on Sept 16? _____

Use with page 34.

Name

Investigation #13: Probing Into
MARVELS OF THE UNIVERSE

What's behind these awesome, wonderful, and mysterious features of the universe?
Do some probing to find out. Then write a brief description or explanation for each one.

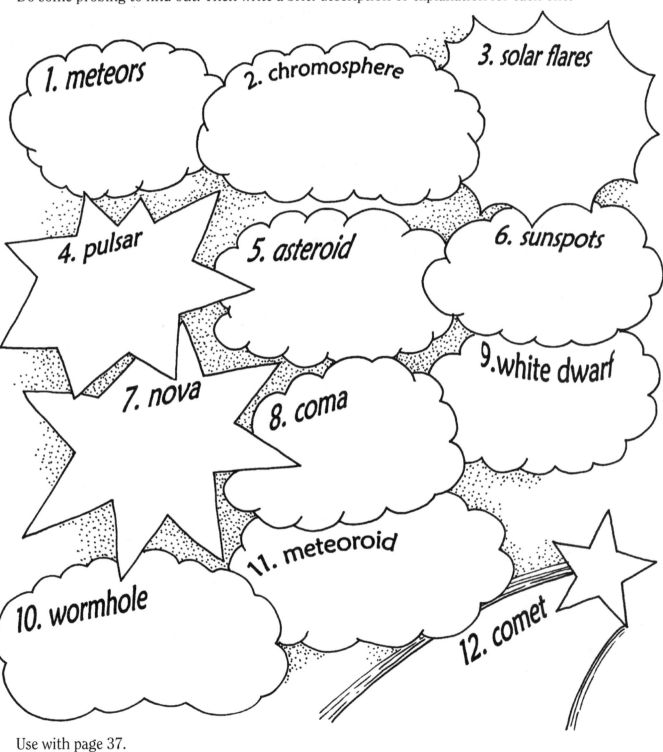

13. binary stars

15. nebulae

14. black hole

17. meteorite

16. shooting star

The Life Story of a Star

18. Write a brief explanation of the birth, life, and death of a star.

Use with page 36.

Name

Investigation #14: Pursuing
PLANETARY PECULIARITIES

Each planet has its own unique features and oddities. No two are alike.

Use good references about space (and all you know about the solar system) as you pursue the peculiarities of the nine *known* planets. Write the name of one or more planets to match each feature described. Use the abbreviations for the planets listed here.

E	Earth
J	Jupiter
M	Mars
MR	Mercury
P	Pluto
N	Neptune
S	Saturn
U	Uranus
V	Venus

_____ 1. These planets have rings.

_____ 2. Its atmosphere is mostly nitrogen and oxygen.

_____ 3. There are ice caps at both poles.

_____ 4. It is the most brilliant body in the sky.

_____ 5. This sphere is drastically tilted—
at 82.1° on its axis.

_____ 6. One of its moons, Europa, was named by Galileo.

_____ 7. It has the most moons.

_____ 8. It is a planet of rocks and ice.

_____ 9. These two planets are the closest to Earth.

_____ 10. Twenty-nine years is the time it takes to orbit the sun.

_____ 11. The planet is often covered by huge dust storms.

_____ 12. It is a blue-green planet.

_____ 13. It is the furthest known planet from the sun.

_____ 14. It takes 88 days to circle the sun.

_____ 15. This is a pale blue planet.

_____ 16. It is 5900 million miles from the sun.

_____ 17. The force of gravity here has less than half
the pull exerted by gravity on Earth.

_____ 18. It is called the red planet because the rocks are
covered with rusty dust.

_____ 19. Its orbital speed is about 30 kilometers per second.

_____ 20. It has two moons.

_____ 21. This is the fastest rotating body in the solar system.

Where am I ?

Use with page 39.

Name

_____ 22. It takes 29 Earth years to travel around the sun one time.

_____ 23. These planets have no moons.

_____ 24. It is the smallest planet known.

_____ 25. Titan is one of its moons.

_____ 26. This planet rotates more slowly than any other.

_____ 27. These planets are mostly "balls of gas."

_____ 28. The length of its day is close to the length of Earth's day.

_____ 29. Rotation takes 10 hours.

_____ 30. It is a colorful, banded planet.

_____ 31. It circles the sun faster than any other planet.

_____ 32. This is closest in size to Earth.

_____ 33. It is the third planet from the sun.

_____ 34. It is called the giant planet.

_____ 35. It is the seventh planet from the sun.

_____ 36. It is the closest planet to the sun.

_____ 37. It is famous for its elaborate system of rings.

_____ 38. It takes 165 years to travel around the sun.

_____ 39. This planet is about half the size of Earth.

_____ 40. It is about 149.6 million miles from the sun.

_____ 41. It takes 59 days to rotate.

_____ 42. The length of a day (daytime and night) is 9 hours.

_____ 43. It has more moons than Jupiter.

_____ 44. It moves around the sun at the slowest speed of any planet.

_____ 45. The trip around the sun takes 84 Earth years.

_____ 46. A thick atmosphere of deadly gasses surrounds this planet.

_____ 47. An asteroid belt is found between the orbits of these two planets.

_____ 48. Only one moon orbits this planet.

Use with page 38.

Name _____

Investigation #15: Inquiring Into
CURIOUS COMBINATIONS

Follow Cathy Lyst around as she investigates some chemical combinations around her house. These are some compounds that make up common substances she uses in her everyday life.

Read the description of each substance. Then do your own investigations to find the chemical formula and the common name for each. Write the missing names and formulas.

1. Cathy washes the hard, calcium carbonate surface of her counters.

2. She adds a cup of sodium hypochlorite to her laundry to whiten and remove stains.

3. While cooking dinner, Cathy adds sodium chloride to her stew to bring out the flavors.

4. She makes fluffy biscuits with the help of sodium hydrogen carbonate.

5. When it is time to eat, she enjoys a nice atmosphere caused by the burning of sticks made of a carbon and hydrogen compound.

6. After dinner, she sweetens her coffee with a compound made of carbon, hydrogen, and oxygen.

7. A compound of carbon and hydrogen burns in her gas heater, keeping the apartment warm.

8. Cathy uses another form of calcium carbonate to write notes to her children on a board in the kitchen.

9. Cathy uses window-cleaning liquid that is a solution of a gas dissolved in water.

Common Name

1. _____

2. _____

3. _____

4. _____

5. _____

6. _____

7. _____

8. _____

9. _____

Formula

1.

2.

3.

4.

5.

6.

7.

8.

9.

Use with page 41.

Name

40

I could do with a few _less_ chemicals in my life right now.

Common Name

Formula

10. Cathy's children love to play outside in the box of silicon dioxide.

11. Cathy is happy when her car has a full supply of this compound of carbon and hydrogen.

12. When she scrapes her arm on the garbage can, Cathy washes the wound thoroughly with a liquid from a brown bottle. It is a compound of hydrogen and oxygen.

13. She soaks a sore ankle in a solution of water and magnesium sulfate hepta-hydrate.

14. Cathy's family members regularly breathe a carbon-oxygen compound into the air in the house.

15. Cathy feeds a spoonful of magnesium hydroxide to her daughter, who has an upset stomach.

16. At the beginning of the summer, Cathy makes sure her car has a good supply of dichlorodifluoromethane.

17. Cathy and her family have a lot of this substance around the house. It is a thick, transparent liquid compound that is used in soap, cosmetics, and inks.

18. Cathy put this compound of calcium oxide on her lawn to help with the growth of new grass seed by reducing the high acidity in the soil.

10. _____ 10. [ ]

11. _____ 11. [ ]

12. _____ 12. [ ]

13. _____ 13. [ ]

14. _____ 14. [ ]

15. _____ 15. [ ]

16. _____ 16. [ ]

17. _____ 17. [ ]

18. _____ 18. [ ]

Use with page 40.

Name _____

Investigation #16: Hunting For
PHYSICS IN THE NEIGHBORHOOD

Whether you know it or not, physics is lurking all around your neighborhood. Sharpen your physics skills and use them to answer these questions.

1. **Why don't people fall out of rollercoasters at the amusement park?**

2. **Why does water run down a bathtub drain in a swirl?**

3. **Why do you weigh more at home than you would on the moon?**

4. **Why is soda pop fizzy?**

5. **Why does a teakettle sing?**

6. **Why is salt added to ice when you're making homemade ice cream in an ice cream freezer?**

Use with page 43.

Name

7. **Why does a suction cup stay on a window?**

11. **Why do you get an electric shock if you touch a doorknob after walking across a carpet?**

8. **Why can you slide faster down a slide when you sit on a plastic or fiberglass mat?**

12. **What makes your milkshake go up your straw?**

9. **How does a sand sculpture keep from falling apart?**

13. **When you row a boat on the pond, why does the boat go forward when you are pulling the oars back toward you?**

10. **Why do you keep moving forward when you slam on the brakes on your bicycle?**

Use with page 42.

Name

Basic Skills/Science Investigations 6-8+

Investigation #17: Discovering
THE SCIENCE BEHIND THE SPORT

Science hangs around every place where sports are happening, whether it's indoors, outdoors, in the air, or underground.

Investigate the science in sports. Choose 3 of the extreme sports listed, and briefly describe a way that science makes the sport possible. Think about the sport's purpose, skills, and equipment.

Lucy runs down a track with a tall, flexible pole until she approaches a sandpile in front of a high bar suspended between two poles. She plants her pole in the sandpile and gives herself a hard push off the ground. The kinetic energy from the running and pushing bends the poles. The kinetic energy is converted for a time into potential energy in the pole. Lucy holds onto the pole while the pole springs back to its original straight shape. As this happens, the potential energy converts into kinetic energy again. This boosts Lucy, clinging to the pole, up into the air. She lets go of the pole, and the inertia keeps her body moving, up and over the bar. Eventually, gravity pulls her downward and she falls to the ground. Thankfully, she lands on a thick, padded mat.

Draw Lucy's Sport

surfing

ski jumping

scuba diving

rafting

snorkeling

windsurfing

snowshoeing

The Sport: _____

The Science: _____

_____

_____

_____

_____

_____

_____

Use with page 45.

Name

hot air ballooning

mountain bike racing

bungee jumping

snowboarding

cross-country skiing

bobsled racing

spelunking (caving)

wakeboarding

water skiing

rock climbing

inline skating

ultimate Frisbee

The Sport: _____

The Science: _____

_____

_____

_____

_____

_____

_____

_____

_____

_____

_____

The Sport: _____

The Science: _____

_____

_____

_____

_____

_____

_____

_____

_____

_____

_____

_____

_____

Use with page 44.

Name _____

Investigation #18: Uncovering
MUSICAL MYSTERIES

Fans of the Splitting Atoms rock band are wild about their music. When the group puts on a concert, how are the musical sounds made? And how do the sounds travel to the fans' ears? Investigate the science of sound to find out.

1. What causes the sounds that come from the drums?_____
   _____
   _____

2. What causes the sounds that come from the voices? _____
   _____
   _____

3. What causes the sounds that come from the guitars and piano?_____
   _____
   _____

4. What causes the sounds that come from the trumpet and the saxophone? _____
   _____

5. How does the sound travel from the band to the fans? _____
   _____

6. Describe a compressional wave. _____
   _____
   _____

7. Define the amplitude of a sound wave. _____
   _____
   _____

8. Define the frequency of sound waves. _____
   _____
   _____

9. What amplitudes of sound waves can be heard by humans?
   _____

10. Which sounds from the bands will have the lowest frequencies—
    high-pitched or low-pitched? _____

Use with page 47.

Name

The band is very loud tonight.

11. Do the sound waves probably have small or large amplitudes?_____

12. Which would be the most likely measurement of the band's loudness?
    (Circle one.)

    3dB   15dB   60dB   115dB

Tonight the band is playing outdoors.

13. It is a cool night. Would the sound travel faster or slower if the temperature were much warmer? _____

14. Is the music likely to sound louder or softer than when the band plays indoors? _____

15. Give an explanation for your answer. _____
    _____
    _____
    _____

During the concert, a jet plane flies over the outdoor stadium.

16. Describe how the Doppler Effect will determine the way the sound of the jet is heard by the fans as it approaches and passes by the stadium.
    _____
    _____
    _____
    _____
    _____

Use with page 46.

Name

Investigation #19: Snooping for
ELUSIVE ELEMENTS

Follow the trail to find the missing elements. Use the Periodic Table (page 50), your knowledge about atomic structure, and your investigative skills to figure out which missing element will fit each clue. Write each element AND its symbol.

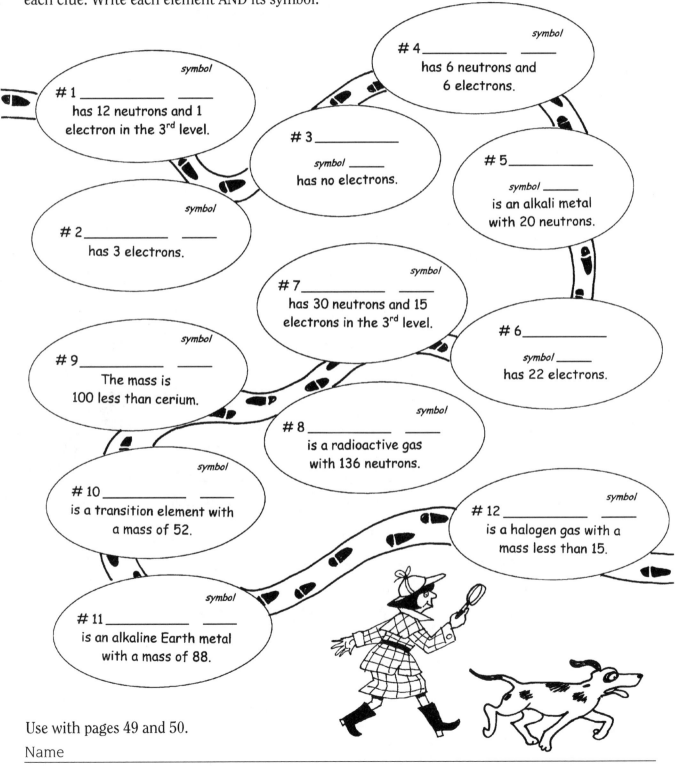

1 _____ _____ *symbol*
has 12 neutrons and 1 electron in the 3rd level.

2 _____ _____ *symbol*
has 3 electrons.

3 _____
symbol _____
has no electrons.

4 _____ _____ *symbol*
has 6 neutrons and 6 electrons.

5 _____
symbol _____
is an alkali metal with 20 neutrons.

6 _____
symbol _____
has 22 electrons.

7 _____ _____ *symbol*
has 30 neutrons and 15 electrons in the 3rd level.

8 _____ _____ *symbol*
is a radioactive gas with 136 neutrons.

9 _____ _____ *symbol*
The mass is 100 less than cerium.

10 _____ _____ *symbol*
is a transition element with a mass of 52.

11 _____ _____ *symbol*
is an alkaline Earth metal with a mass of 88.

12 _____ _____ *symbol*
is a halogen gas with a mass less than 15.

Use with pages 49 and 50.

Name _____

Basic Skills/Science Investigations 6-8+

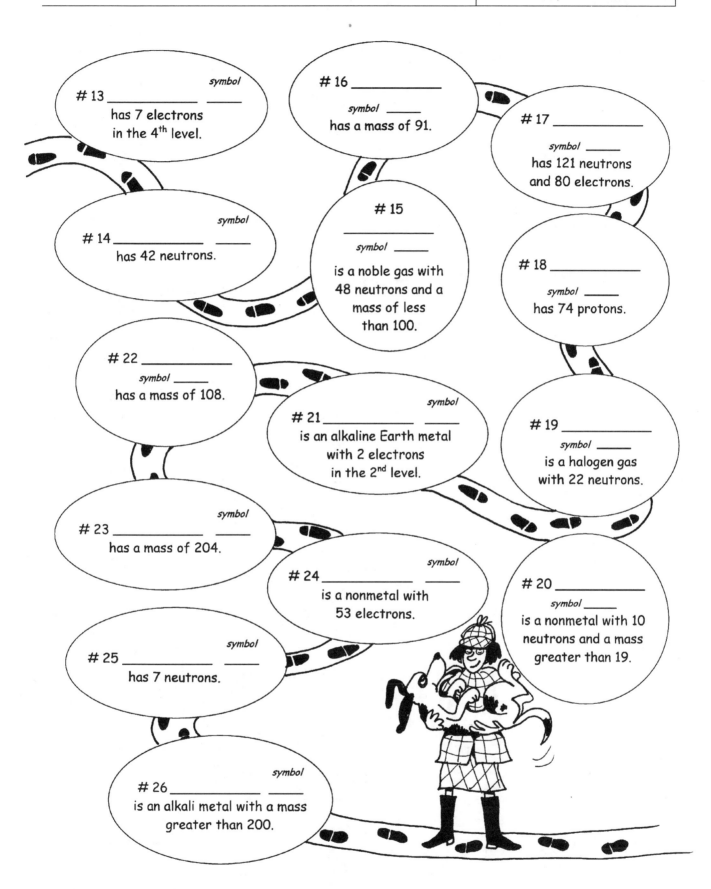

13 _____ _____
symbol
has 7 electrons
in the 4th level.

16 _____
symbol _____
has a mass of 91.

17 _____
symbol _____
has 121 neutrons
and 80 electrons.

14 _____ _____
symbol
has 42 neutrons.

15
_____
symbol _____
is a noble gas with
48 neutrons and a
mass of less
than 100.

18 _____
symbol _____
has 74 protons.

22 _____
symbol _____
has a mass of 108.

21 _____ _____
symbol
is an alkaline Earth metal
with 2 electrons
in the 2nd level.

19 _____
symbol _____
is a halogen gas
with 22 neutrons.

23 _____ _____
symbol
has a mass of 204.

24 _____
symbol
is a nonmetal with
53 electrons.

20 _____
symbol _____
is a nonmetal with 10
neutrons and a mass
greater than 19.

25 _____
symbol
has 7 neutrons.

26 _____
symbol
is an alkali metal with a mass
greater than 200.

Use with pages 48 and 50.

Name

Basic Skills/Science Investigations 6-8+

PERIODIC TABLE

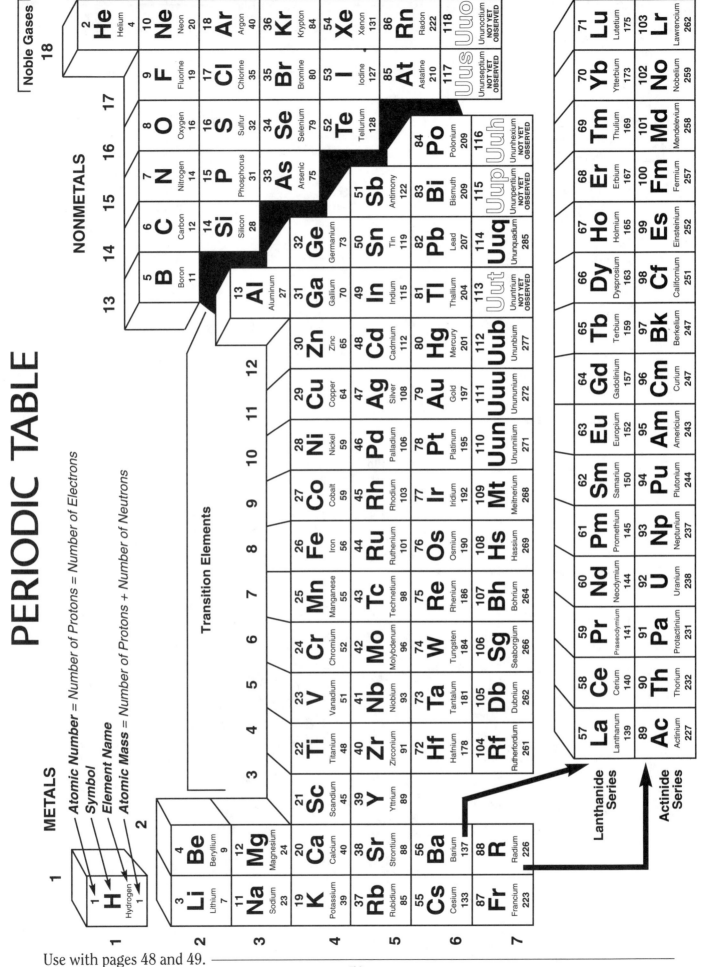

Atomic Number = Number of Protons = Number of Electrons
Symbol
Element Name
Atomic Mass = Number of Protons + Number of Neutrons

METALS

NONMETALS

Noble Gases

Transition Elements

Lanthanide Series

Actinide Series

APPENDIX

CONTENTS

TERMS FOR SCIENCE INVESTIGATIONS

abrasion — process in which wind carries fine particles that scour rock surfaces

acid — a substance that produces hydronium ions when dissolved in water

alkaline metal — the family of elements in Group 2 of the Periodic Table, very reactive

amplitude — the greatest distance the particles in a wave rise or fall from their rest position

angiosperm — a seed plant that produces seeds inside a fruit; a flowering plant

antibiotic — a substance produced by a living organism that slows down or stops the growth of bacteria

antihistamine — a compound used in treating allergic reactions

antiseptic — a substance that sterilizes and kills germs

aurora borealis — streams of light in the upper atmosphere near the North Pole

aurora australias — streams of light in the upper atmosphere near the South Pole

base — a substance that increases the hydroxide ion concentration when added to water

centripetal force — a force on an object operating toward the center of a circular path

chemistry — the study of matter, its composition and its changes

chemotherapy — use of chemical agents in the treatment or control of disease

comet — a mass of frozen gases, dust particles, and rock particles that orbits the sun

compressional wave — a wave in which matter vibrates in the same direction the wave moves

Coriolis effect — the apparent deflection of a moving object that is the result of the Coriolis force

Coriolis force — An apparent force that as a result of the earth's rotation deflects moving objects (as projectiles or currents) to the right in the northern hemisphere and to the left in the southern hemisphere

cytology — the study of cells

deep water wave — a wave moving in water that is deeper than one-half its wavelength

deflation — process in which wind picks up loose material from the ground surface and moves it

density currents — currents formed by the movement of more dense water toward an area of less dense water

Doppler effect — a change in the frequency of sound waves due to the movement of the listener or the object making the sound

eclipse — the passing of one object into the shadow of another object

endocrinology — the study of the endocrine system

epidemiologist — a scientist who studies disease

exoskeleton — the hard outer covering protecting inner organs of an arthropod

fault — a fracture in a rock along which movement has taken place

fission — splitting or breaking into parts

flagellum — the whip-like tail on some simple-celled animals that helps in movement

floodplain — sediment dropped outside the river bed during flooding

frequency — the number of waves that pass a given point per second

fusion — the joining together of parts into a whole

friction — a force that opposes motion between two surfaces that touch each other

halogen gases — elements in Group 17 on the Periodic Table; reactive nonmetals

hematology — the study of blood

Basic Skills/Science Investigations 6-8+

inertia — the property of a body that resists any change in velocity

kinetic energy — energy of motion

kingdom — the major classification category of living organisms

landslides — quick movement of large amounts of material down hills

loess — unstratified buff to yellowish brown soil believed to be chiefly deposited by the wind

meteor — a meteoroid that burns up entering Earth's atmosphere

meteorite — a meteor that reaches the Earth's surface without being completely vaporized

meteoroid — matter in orbit around the sun that is outside the earth's atmosphere

mineral — a naturally occurring, inorganic, crystalline solid with a definite chemical make-up

momentum — the product of an object's mass and its velocity

mudflows — rapid movement of soil from weathering mixed with rain down a slope

neap tide — low tide that occurs when the sun, Earth, and moon form a right angle

nebulae — clouds of dust and gas where stars are born

organism — a living thing

phylum — the largest classification category in a kingdom

pitch — a quality of sound (highness or lowness) determined by wave frequency

podiatry — the medical treatment of feet

potential energy — energy due to position or condition

pulsar — rapidly rotating neutron star that gives out a beam of radiation which looks like a pulse

quarantine — to separate an organism from others

quark — a subatomic particle

revolution — the movement of a body (or object) around another body (or object)

rotation — the turning or spinning of an object on an axis

seismic waves — vibrations set up by earthquakes

shallow water wave — a wave in water shallower than one-half its wavelength

shooting star — a briefly visible meteor

solar flares — sudden increases in brightness of the sun's chromosphere

species — biological classification ranking below the genus comprising related organisms or populations

spring tide — a tide that occurs when the sun, moon, and Earth are aligned

static electricity — electricity produced by charged bodies; charge built up in one place

sunspots — dark spots on the sun where the temperature is cooler

talus — eroded material that collects at the foot of a steep slope or cliff

tides — shallow water waves caused by the gravitational attraction among Earth, moon, and sun

till — unsorted, unlayered glacial deposit of boulders, sand, and clay

transitional elements — elements in Groups 3–12 on the Periodic Table; most have two electrons in the outer energy level

tropism — the response of a plant to a stimulus

vacuole — a liquid-filled sac in a cell; stores water and other material

velocity — the speed and direction of a moving object

vibrations — rapid movements back and forth

wormhole — theoretical tunnels that link one part of space-time with another

53

PHYSICAL PROPERTIES OF SOME COMMON MINERALS

Metallic Luster

Mineral	Color	Streak	Hardness	Crystals
GRAPHITE	black to gray	black to gray	1-2	hexagonal
SILVER	silvery, white	light gray to silver	2.5	cubic
GALENA	gray	gray to black	2.5	cubic
GOLD	pale golden-yellow	yellow	2.5-3	cubic
COPPER	copper red	copper red	3	cubic
CHROMITE	black or brown	brown to black	5.5	cubic
MAGNETITE	black	black	6	cubic
PYRITE	light brassy yellow	greenish black	6.5	cubic

Nonmetallic Luster

Mineral	Color	Streak	Hardness	Crystals
TALC	white, greenish	white	1	monoclinic
GYPSUM	colorless, gray, white	white	2	monoclinic
SULFUR	yellow	yellow to white	2	orthorhombic
MUSCOVITE	white, gray, yellow, rose, green	colorless	2.5	basal cleavage
HALITE	colorless, red, white, blue	colorless	2.5	cubic
CALCITE	colorless, white	colorless, white	3	hexagonal
DOLOMITE	colorless, white, pink, green, gray	white	3.5-4	hexagonal
FLOURITE	colorless, white, blue, green, red, yellow, purple	colorless	4	cubic
HORNBLENDE	green to black	gray to white	5-6	monoclinic
FELDSPAR	gray, green, white	colorless	6	monoclinic
QUARTZ	colorless, colors	colorless	7	hexagonal
GARNET	yellow-red, green, black	colorless	7.5	cubic
TOPAZ	white, pink, yellow, blue, colorless	colorless	8	orthorhombic
CORUNDUM	colorless, blue, brown	colorless	9	hexagonal
DIAMOND	colorless, dark, many colors	colorless	10	octagonal or hexagonal

Moh's Hardness Scale

Mineral	Hardness	Hardness Test
TALC	1	softest, can be scratched by a fingernail
GYPSUM	2	soft, can be scratched by a fingernail but cannot be scratched by talc
CALCITE	3	can be scratched by a penny
FLOURITE	4	can be scratched by a steel knife or a nail file
APATITE	5	can be scratched by a steel knife or nail file, but not easily
FELDSPAR	6	knife cannot scratch it; it can scratch glass
QUARTZ	7	scratches glass and steel
TOPAZ	8	can scratch quartz
CORUNDUM	9	can scratch topaz
DIAMOND	10	can scratch all others

SOME PARTICULARS ABOUT PLANETS

Planet	Average Distance from the Sun in Millions of Kilometers	Average Orbital Speed in Kilometers per second	Diameter at Equator in kilometers	Mass (in comparison to Earth—Earth being 1)	Length of Rotation (in Earth days)	Length of Revolution	Number of Known Satellites
Mercury	57.9	48	4880	0.055	59 days	88 days	0
Venus	108.2	35	12,100	.0815	243 days Retrograde Motion	224.7 days	0
Earth	149.6	30	12,756	1	23 hours, 56 minutes	365 days	1
Mars	227.9	24	6,794	0.107	24 hours, 37 minutes	687 days	2
Jupiter	778.3	13	142,984	317.9	9 hours, 55 minutes	11.86 years	16
Saturn	1,429	9.6	120,536	95.2	10 hours, 39 minutes	29.46 years	17
Uranus	2,875	6.8	51,100	14.54	17.3 hours Retrograde Motion	84 years	15
Neptune	4,504	5.4	49,200	17.2	17 hours, 50 minutes	165 years	2
Pluto	5,900	4.7	3200 (?)	.002	8 days, 9 hours Retrograde Motion	248 years	1

HOW FAR DID YOU SAY IT WAS FROM URANUS TO MARS?

Basic Skills/Science Investigations 6-8+

SCIENCE INVESTIGATIONS
SKILLS TEST

Each answer is worth one point. Total possible points = 70

1–8: Write T for each true statement and F for each false statement.

_____ 1. A substance that has excess OH^+ ions will turn blue litmus paper red.

_____ 2. A quark is a subatomic particle.

_____ 3. You could see an aurora borealis in Argentina or Borneo.

_____ 4. In the light spectrum, the red waves are shorter than the blue waves.

_____ 5. Fresh water has greater density than saltwater.

_____ 6. About 50% of Earth's surface is water.

_____ 7. Vacuoles are structures for storing food and water in living cells.

_____ 8. Sharks and squids squirt a dark ink to protect themselves from predators.

9–20: Write an answer to each question. (Not all answers are found on the signs.)

_____ 9. This is the phylum of a zebra.

_____ 10. Bacteria belong to this kingdom.

_____ 11. This is the phylum of sponges.

_____ 12. A mouse belongs to this class.

_____ 13. This is the kingdom of a euglenoid.

_____ 14. Roundworms belong to this phylum.

_____ 15. A tarantula, lobster, and ladybug share this phylum.

_____ 16. Daddy Longlegs, ticks, and mites belong to this class.

_____ 17. Starfish, sea cucumbers, and sea urchins share this phylum.

_____ 18. A snail, slug, squid, octopus, and oyster share this phylum.

_____ 19. A jellyfish, sea anemone, hydra, and coral share this phylum.

_____ 20. Algae, horsetails, and liverworts belong to this kingdom.

Kingdoms
Protist
Moneran
Fungus
Plant
Animal

Animal Phyla
Porifera
Coelenteratata
Platyhelminthes
Nematoda
Annelida
Mollusca
Arthropoda
Echinodermata
Chordata

Name _____

21–23: Write each answer in the box containing each question.

21. What causes a shiver?	22. Why does water swirl down a bathtub drain?	23. Why don't people fall out of a rollercoaster?
	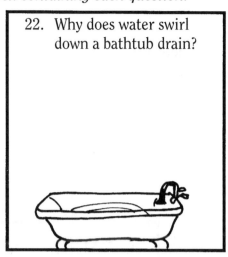	

24–33. Circle one or more correct answers for each question.

24. Which of these ailments is NOT likely to be treated with antibiotics?
   a. pneumonia   c. diabetes   e. shock
   b. hypothermia   d. anthrax   f. ankle sprain

25. Which is true of sharks?
   a. They are predators.   c. They have smooth skin.
   b. They have bones.   d. They are carnivores.

26. Which is a large salivary gland?
   a. parotid   b. thymus   c. thyroid   d. pituitary   e. hypothalamus

27. Which organ stores bile in the human body?
   a. the spleen   b. the liver   c. the gallbladder   d. the stomach

28. What regulates the human heartbeat?
   a. the medulla   b. the cerebrum   c. the spinal cord   d. the cerebellum

29. What secretes a substance that regulates glucose in the human body?
   a. the sciatic nerve   b. the dendrites   c. the adrenal glands   d. the pancreas

30. What weather condition is characterized by a warm, moist air mass behind held close to the ground by a heavier, colder air mass above it?
   a. sleet   b. fog   c. hail   d. a cyclone   e. a strong gale

31. What is the amplitude of sound waves that can be heard by humans?
   a. 20–20,000 Mz   b. 200–200,000 Mz   c. 20–2000 Mz

32. A collapsed star from which no light can escape is a
   a. black hole.   c. pulsar.   e. red giant.
   b. wormhole.   d. white dwarf.   f. nova.

33. While Mrs. Laze lounges, sunbathing in her yard, the neighbor mows his lawn. Which is true about the sound Mrs. Laze as the mower approaches her chair?
   a. The waves compress together.   d. The waves have a higher frequency.
   b. The waves get farther apart.   e. The pitch gets higher.
   c. The waves have a lower frequency.   f. The pitch gets lower.

Name

34–37: Write the answer.

34. What blood types can donate to AB negative? _____

35. To which blood types can an A type donate? _____

36. Does sound travel faster through cold air or warm air?_____

37. Of what materials is a comet composed? _____

38–45: Write the letter that shows the correct chemical formula for each compound.

_____ 38. baking soda

_____ 39. candle wax

_____ 40. sugar

_____ 41. ammonia

_____ 42. bleach

_____ 43. sand

_____ 44. salt

_____ 45. chalk

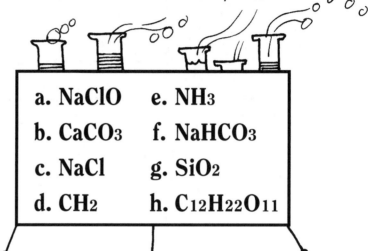

a. NaClO   e. NH_3

b. $CaCO_3$ f. $NaHCO_3$

c. NaCl   g. SiO_2

d. CH_2 h. $C_{12}H_{22}O_{11}$

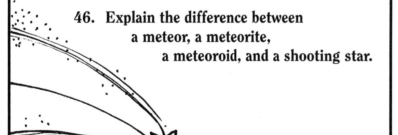

46. **Explain the difference between a meteor, a meteorite, a meteoroid, and a shooting star.**

47–51. Circle the numbers of the statements that are true.

47. Saturn, Uranus, and Jupiter have rings.

48. Mars is the only planet with polar ice caps.

49. Mars and Venus are the closest planets to Earth.

50. Jupiter is the fastest rotating planet.

51. Mercury is the closest planet to the sun.

Name _____

52–58: Name the earth surface feature or process that matches each description.

_____ 52. Slow-flowing basalt erupts from vents in the Earth's surface to form this volcano.

_____ 53. Movement takes place along a fracture in Earth's surface.

_____ 54. Material pulled downward by gravity collects at the foot of a steep slope.

_____ 55. A flooding river deposits fine sediment outside of the river channel.

_____ 56. A moving glacier picks up debris and moves it to other places.

_____ 57. Steam pressure forces water through an opening in the crust at regular intervals.

_____ 58. Wind picks up loose material from the surface and moves it around.

59. This rock hound has found a chunk of a mineral.
   It is white, non-metallic, and can be scratched by a fingernail.
   Which of these could it be? *(Circle one or more.)*

   talc   **halite**   **calcite**

   quartz   **gypsum**   **galena**   **diamond**

60. Which statements about ocean water are true? *(Circle one or more answers.)*
   a. Cold water is more dense than warm water.
   b. Increased salinity decreases density.
   c. Water moves from an area of greater density to lesser density.

61. Which statements are true of a spring tide? *(Circle one or more answers.)*
   a. Gravitational pull of the Earth, moon, and sun are lined up.
   b. High tides are at their highest and low tides are at their lowest.
   c. There is a smaller tidal range than during neap tides.

62–66: Name the element indicated
   by each symbol below.

_____ 62. He

_____ 63. Mn

_____ 64. Ag

_____ 65. Hg

_____ 66. Na

13

Al

27

_____ 67. What is this element?

_____ 68. What is the mass?

_____ 69. What is the atomic number?

_____ 70. How many electrons are in the 3rd level?

SCORE: Total Points _____ out of a possible 70 points

Name

SCIENCE INVESTIGATIONS
SKILLS TEST ANSWER KEY

1. F
2. T
3. F
4. F
5. F
6. F
7. T
8. F
9. chordata
10. moneran
11. porifera
12. mammal
13. protist
14. nematoda
15. arthropoda
16. arachnid
17. echinodermata
18. mollusca
19. coelenterata
20. plant
21. Muscles contract involuntarily to release chemicals that produce heat and keep the body warm.
22. Earth's rotation causes the swirling.
23. Inertia and centripetal forces keep people pushed back in their seats.
24. b, c, e, f
25. a, d
26. a
27. c
28. a
29. d
30. b
31. a
32. a
33. a, d, e
34. A negative, B negative, AB negative, and O negative

35. A and AB
36. warm
37. ice, dust, dirt
38. f
39. d
40. h
41. e
42. a
43. g
44. c
45. b
46. Meteoroid: .... small fragment of matter moving in space (or small pieces of asteroids)
    Meteor: .... meteoroid that burns up in Earth's atmosphere
    Meteorite: .... meteor that strikes Earth
    Shooting Star: ..... briefly visible meteor
47–51: Numbers 49, 50, and 51 should be circled.
52. shield volcano
53. fault
54. talus
55. flood plain
56. plucking or till
57. geyser
58. loess or deflation
59. talc, halite, calcite, gypsum
60. a, c
61. a, b
62. helium
63. manganese
64. silver
65. mercury
66. sodium
67. aluminum
68. 27
69. 13
70. 17

ANSWERS

Pages 10–13

Answers will vary. Those shown here offer basic guidelines against which to check answers. Web addresses will vary.

1. no
2. Most of the wavelengths from light pass through the air. The short, blue waves get scattered around the sky so it is the blue color that reaches the eyes.
3. visible comets depend on year and season (answers will vary)
4. acid has excess H+ ions and turns blue litmus red; base has excess OH+ ions and turns red litmus blue
5. vacuoles store food or water in the cells
6. epidemics
7. no
8. Cats ingest hair from cleaning their fur. Fur cannot be digested, so they cough it up.
9. a protein called keratin
10. 25 million years (approximately)
11. Do not struggle. Use slow swimming movements, float on top and roll to solid ground.
12. 2½ billion times (approximately)
13. no
14. camels (also: alpaca, guanaco, vicuña)
15. they are in an orbit—a combination of speed and altitude that keeps them circling instead of being pulled down by Earth's gravity
16. in an atom
17. salt water is heavier (more dense) than fresh water
18. the force that affects anything moving through air and makes it turn slightly—because the Earth is rotating
19. borealis is seen in northern hemisphere; australis is seen in southern hemisphere
20. New England, Midwest, southwest deserts, or Southeast

21. fission splits atoms apart; fusion joins atoms
22. forces between the water molecules pull them apart
23. 326 million cubic miles–70% of Earth's surface
24. good, hard material for building; many monuments are made of granite

Pages 14–15

1. yes; plant
2. no; plant
3. porifera; animal
4. moneran
5. yes; animal
6. coelenterata; animal
7. yes; arthropoda; animal
8. yes; arthropoda; animal
9. protist
10. arachnid; arthropoda; animal
11. nematoda (roundworms); animal
12. echinodermata; animal; clam
13. carnivore; mammal; chordata; animal
14. fern; plant
15. fungus or fungi
16. snail, oyster, slug, squid, and clam; mollusca; animal

Pages 16–17

Answers may vary somewhat.
1. every 12–37 years
2. silica (sand)
3. Little hairs are triggered by the fly, making the plant spring shut.
4. sweet nectar near the top, slippery sides
5. duckweed; on ponds
6. seeds are huge-weighing up to 50 pounds
7. They attach their roots to fungi that are already attached to tree roots.
8. It attaches itself to the roots of other plants.
9. The bottom of each frond holds up to a quart of water.
10. The smell attracts flies to pollinate the plant.
11. shape of a bucket
12. they surround a tree and acquire nutrients from it, in the process they grow so fast that they suffocate or strangle the tree.
13. Its leaves line up in a north-south direction.

14. The plant dries out but turns green again when water is available.

Page 18

1. 4 of the following: A, B, C, D, E, G, H, L, M, N, O, P
2. M
3. A, D, E, H, O, P
4. B
5. T
6. N
7. S
8. C
9. L
10. G
11. F
12. Q

Page 19

1–24. The following numbers should be circled to show true statements: 2, 3, 7, 8, 9, 12, 13, 16, 17, 19, 22, 23, 24
A. sharp spines with poisonous venom
B. They have razor-sharp teeth.

Pages 20–21

1. Dr. G Larynx
   auditory nerve; gallbladder; hemoglobin; thyroid; sciatic nerves
2. Dr. L. Bowe
   dentine; pancreas; thymus; iliac; external obliques
3. Dr. A. Orta
   platelets; gastrocnemius; bronchi; Fallopian tubes; jugular veins
4. Dr. S. Turnam
   iris; metatarsals; medulla; melanin; deltoid
5. Dr. B. J. Renal
   spleen; dendrites; ventricles; bile; parotid

Pages 22–23

1. She has sleep residue in the corners of her eyes.
2. She has hiccups.
3. She is burping.
4. She sneezed.
5. She has dandruff.
6. She is snoring.
A–G. Answers may vary.
A. The protective, waterproof layer on the skin (keratin) absorbs water and stretches

out to form wrinkles (particularly on hands and feet where the keratin layer is thickest).
B. The ulnar nerve runs from the shoulder to the hand, passing over the elbow. When it is pinched between the bone and a hard surface, the nerve sends a signal of pain to the brain.
C. When the brain or body needs more oxygen, a reflex action causes an inhalation of air that forces oxygen into the lungs.
D. Odor caused from chemicals in foods or from bacteria in the mouth
E. Air pressure changes when a plane ascends or descends. Eardrums bulge or sink because the pressure in the inner ear is different from that outside. The Eustachian tubes eventually open up and allow air in or out to equalize the pressure. This returns the eardrum to its normal position with a "pop."
F. Muscles involuntarily contract to release chemicals which produce heat and warm the body. This is a reflex response to cold.
G. It is cerumen that coats the ear canal, produced by glands in the ear canal to catch dust and debris and protect the ears against germs.

Pages 24–25

Answers will vary according to diseases chosen. Review student responses to see that they are sensible.

Page 26

1. seismic waves—vibrations set up by sudden movement of Earth surface rocks (earthquakes)
2. strato-volcano—flows of lava, ash, cinders and rock fragments erupting through a vent in Earth's surface
3. caldera—valley at the top of a volcanic peak caused when the volcano becomes hollow and collapses, or when the top is blown during an eruption

Answers

4. fault—movement that takes place along fractures in Earth's surface
5. dome volcano—slow-flowing rhyolite erupts from a crack or vent in Earth's surface
6. hot springs—water, heated by intrusive igneous rock or magma beneath the surface, bubbles unrestricted to the surface
7. folding—compressional forces move rock layers from horizontal position to bends
8. shield volcano—slow-flowing basalt erupts from vents in Earth's surface
9. geyser—hot springs with a small surface opening, through which the heated water is forced upward at regular intervals by steam pressure beneath the surface

Page 27

Answers will vary depending upon the source of information.
1. 700; 8.3
2. 160,000; 7.5
3. Kansu, China; 200,000; 8.6
4. 143,000; 8.3
5. 200,000; 8.3
6. Kansu, China; 70,000; 7.6
7. Quetta, India; 50,000; 7.5
8. 110,000; 7.3
9. 131; 9.2
10. 66,000; 7.8
11. 23,000; 7.5
12. Tang-Shan, China; 225,000; 8.0
13. 55,000; 7.0
14. San Francisco, CA; 62; 7.1
15. 40,000; 7.7
16. 61; 6.8
17. Kobe, Japan; 5502; 7.2
18. 4700; 7.9
19. 30,000; 7.4
20. 20,000; 7.7
21. An earthquake consists of vibrations caused by sudden movement in surface rocks.

Pages 28–29

1. deflation
2. abrasion
3. loess
4. Dunes
5. talus
6. rock fall
7. Landslides
8. mudslides or mudflows
9. creep
10. alluvial fans
11. suspended; bed
12. levee; floodplain
13. delta
14. caves or caverns; natural; sinkholes
15. abrading; striations
16. plucking
17. till; moraines

Pages 30–31

1. halite
2. garnet
3. pyrite
4. calcite
5. gypsum
6. quartz
7. galena
8. topaz
9. corundum
10. graphite
11. copper
12. sulfur
13. magnetite
14. talc
15. diamond
16. silver

Pages 32–33

Explanations may differ somewhat.
1. winds
2. differences in water density due to differences in temperature and salinity of water
3. winds, tides, and earthquakes
4. Each water particle moves in a circle within the wave.
5. In a deep-water wave the water is deeper than $\frac{1}{2}$ the wavelength; in a shallow-water wave, the water is shallower than $\frac{1}{2}$ the wavelength.
6. The top of a wave moves faster than the bottom of the wave, so the wave gets lopsided and collapses.
7. breaking waves
8. The surfer must paddle to move as fast as a coming wave. When the wave picks up the board, the surfer must guide the board to stay ahead of the crest of the wave.
9. The gravitational attraction among Earth, moon and sun. The forces pulling cause a bulge in the ocean water on the side of Earth facing the moon. The rotational force of the Earth and moon cause another bulge to form on the side of the Earth opposite the moon.

Diagrams on page 33:

1. spring tide; high tides are highest and low tides are lowest—with greatest tidal range (Moon's, sun's, and Earth's gravitational pull are all lined up.)
2. spring tide; high tides are highest and low tides are lowest—with greatest tidal range (Moon's, sun's, and Earth's gravitational pull are all lined up.)
3. neap tide; tides are minimal—with lesser tidal range (Moon's, sun's, and Earth's gravitational pull are not lined up, but pulling in different directions.)
4. neap tide; tides are minimal—with lesser tidal range (Moon's, sun's, and Earth's gravitational pull are not lined up, but pulling in different directions.)

Pages 34–35

1. cooling effect of wind takes the heat from the body, making the temperature feel colder than it is
2. snowstorms with high winds
3. overflowing of water onto land that is normally dry
4. raindrops falling through a layer of air colder than –3° C, causing raindrops to freeze
5. strong wind carrying clouds of sand through the air
6. name given to hurricanes in the southwest Pacific Ocean and the South China Sea
7. heavy rainy season in areas of India, South Asia, West Africa, and Northern Australia
8. heavy rains and high winds
9. ice crystals are tossed up and down in the cloud, water freezes in crystals in layers
10. tornado formed over the sea
11. intense heating of air caused it to rise and form large cumulonimbus clouds with heavy rain, lightning, and thunder
12. funnel-shaped storm; strong rotating column of air reaching from a cumulonimbus cloud to the ground
13. warm low pressure weather system surrounded by cooler air
14. hurricane conditions are possible in a specified area within the next 36 hours
15. hurricane conditions are expected in specified area within 24 hours
16. tropical cyclone—storm with great energy and winds over 75 mph
17. hurricane with winds between 130–155 mph
18. long period without precipitation
19. warm, moist air mass near the ground covered and held down by heavier mass of cold air
20. wind of between 47 and 54 mph
A. no
B. yes
C. no

Pages 36–37

1. meteoroids that have reached Earth's atmosphere
2. bright red layer of sun's surface, which contains hydrogen gas
3. sudden increases in brightness of the sun's chromosphere
4. rapidly rotating neutron star gives out a beam of radiation that looks like a pulse
5. fragments of matter orbiting the sun, similar material to material in planets
6. dark spots on the sun where temperatures are colder
7. a star suddenly exploding with increased brightness
8. large halo of dust and gas formed around the nucleus of a comet
9. star that has collapsed after using all its fuel
10. theoretical tunnels that link one part of space-time with another

Basic Skills/Science Investigations 6-8+   Copyright ©2003 by Incentive Publications, Inc., Nashville, TN.

11. small piece of asteroid material flying in space

12. balls of soot, dust, and ice that orbit the sun; as they get close to the sun, they turn to steam, showing a long tail

13. two stars orbiting a common center of gravity

14. a collapsed star from which no light can escape

15. clouds of dust and gas where stars are born

16. briefly visible meteor

17. meteor that strikes Earth's surface

18. (Explanations may vary somewhat.) A star is born inside a cloud of gas and dust. Gravity condenses some of the cloud into a red protostar. Spinning flattens this into a disk. The contractions heat the core and set off nuclear reactions that make the star shine. The star shines for millions of years until the fuel is used up. Then the core contracts, and the outer layers swell to a red giant. Eventually outer layers expand into space, leaving a white dwarf. Then it cools and leaves a cinder, called a black dwarf.

Pages 38–39

1. S, U	25. S
2. E	26. V
3. M	27. J, U, N, S
4. J	28. M
5. U	29. S
6. J	30. J
7. S	31. MR
8. P	32. V
9. M, V	33. E
10. S	34. J
11. M	35. U
12. U (N optional)	36. MR
13. P	37. S
14. MR	38. N
15. N	39. M
16. P	40. E
17. MR	41. MR
18. M	42. J
19. E	43. S
20. M	44. P
21. J	45. U
22. S	46. V
23. V, M	47. M, J
24. P	48. P, E

Pages 40–41

1. marble; $CaCo_3$
2. bleach; $NaClO$
3. salt; $NaCl$
4. baking soda; $NaHCo_3$
5. candle wax; CH_2
6. sugar; $C_{12}H_{22}O_{11}$
7. natural gas or methane; $CH4$
8. chalk; $CaCo_3$
9. ammonia; NH_3
10. sand; SiO_2
11. gasoline; C_8H_{18}
12. hydrogen peroxide; H_2O_2
13. Epsom's salt
14. carbon dioxide; CO_2
15. milk of magnesia; $Mg(OH)_2$
16. Freon; CF_2Cl_2
17. glycerin
18. lime; CaO

Pages 42–43

1. The inertia and centripetal force keeps everyone pushed back into their seats.

2. because of the spinning of the Earth

3. Gravity pulls down on a person with more force on Earth than on the moon.

4. As water heats, small particles turn to bubbles of steam. The bubbles float up and hit colder water. The bubbles collapse or pop with a noise. Hundreds of popping bubbles cause a noise that sounds like singing.

5. It is a solution of liquid and a gas, CO_2. The gas causes the fizz.

6. The salt lowers the freezing temperature of the water (or ice), making the temperature cold enough to be able to freeze the cream.

7. When the suction cup is squeezed, some of the air is removed. When the cup is placed against the window, the air pressure outside the cup is greater than inside the cup. This pressure holds the cup against the window.

8. The mat reduces the friction that slows down movement.

9. Sand sculptures are made with wet sand. The water added to sand makes the molecules adhere to each other. The force of cohesion also causes molecules of the sand to stick together.

10. The first law of motion—inertia keeps a body moving in the same direction and at the same rate; *or* an object resists a change in velocity

11. Static electricity has built up in your body from rubbing against the carpet.

12. When you suck on the straw, you reduce the air pressure in the straw. Then, the pressure above the liquid is greater than the pressure inside the straw, so the liquid is pressed up into the straw.

13. The third law of motion: for every force there is an equal and opposite force; OR action-reaction causes the boat to move in the opposite direction from the force of the pull.

Pages 44–45

Lucy's sport is pole vaulting. Student should draw this sport. Other answers will vary depending on the sports chosen. Check to see that student answers are accurate and reasonable.

Pages 46–47

1. vibrations of drum surfaces setting up sound waves

2. vibrations of vocal cords setting up sound waves

3. vibrations of the strings in the instruments

4. vibrations of columns of air in the instruments

5. through the air in waves

6. a wave in which the matter vibrates in the same direction that the wave moves

7. the greatest distance wave particles travel in rising or falling from their resting position

8. number of waves that pass a point in a given amount of time

9. Answer may vary slightly depending on the source: 20–20,000 HZ (megahertz)

10. low pitched

11. large

12. 115dB

13. faster

14. softer

15. Indoors there are surfaces that bounce sound waves back to the ear.

16. As the jet approaches, the sound waves compress together more tightly, so waves have a higher frequency and a higher pitched sound. As the jet passes, sound waves get farther apart, so the waves have lower frequency and the sound has a lower pitch.

Pages 48–49

1. sodium; Na
2. lithium, Li
3. hydrogen; H
4. carbon; C
5. potassium; K
6. titanium; Ti
7. manganese, Mn
8. radon; Rn
9. calcium, Ca
10. chromium; Ca
11. strontium; Sr
12. helium; He
13. bromine; Br
14. arsenic; As
15. krypton; Kr
16. zirconium; Zr
17. mercury, Hg
18. tungsten; W
19. argon; Ar
20. neon; Ne
21. beryllium; Be
22. silver; Ag
23. thallium; Tl
24. iodine; I
25. nitrogen; N
26. francium; Fr